# BEARS
## 51 Fascinating, Crazy & Weird Facts
### By TJ Rob

**From the Fascinating, Crazy and Weird Animal Facts Series, Volume 1**

### Copyright:

Copyright Text TJ Rob, 2016

All rights reserved. No part of the book may be reproduced in any form without permission in writing from the author. Reviewers may quote brief passages in review.

ISBN 978-1-988695-36-5

### Disclaimer:

No part of this book may be reproduced in any form or by any means, mechanical or electronic, including photocopying or recording, or by an information storage and retrieval system, or transmitted by email without permission in writing from the publisher. This book is for entertainment purposes only. The views expressed are those of the author alone.

### Published by:

TJ Rob - www.TJRob.com
Suite 609
440-10816 Macleod Trail SE
Calgary, AB T2J 5N8

### Photo Credits:

Images used under license from Shutterstock.com, Flickr.com, Pixabay.com, Creative Commons, Wikimedia Commons and Public Domain.
Front Cover – Photo By Rob Annis / Flickr.com, Back Cover – Photo By KIUKO / Flickr.com; Title Page - Image by DigitalDesigner / Pixabay.com

# Table of Contents:

1. How many species of Bears are there?....................................................................4
2. Where do you find Bears today?..........................................................................5
3. How fast can Bears run?....................................................................................6
4. Is a Polar Bear's fur really white?......................................................................7
5. What color skin do Polar Bears have?..................................................................8
6. Do Polar Bears favor one giant paw over the other?...............................................9
7. Can the biggest Bear jump?..............................................................................10
8. How far do Polar Bears roam?..........................................................................11
9. How much can a Polar Bear eat?.......................................................................12
10. How are the names "Arctic" and "Antarctic" connected to Bears? .............13
11. What are the only true meat-eating Bears?......................................................14
12. Does a Polar Bear have a cloak of invisibility? ................................................15
13. Are Koala Bears really Bears?........................................................................16
14. Are Giant Panda Bears endangered?...............................................................17
15. What human illnesses do Giant Panda Bears suffer from?..................................18
16. What do Giant Pandas eat a ton of?................................................................19
17. Do Giant Pandas bite?...................................................................................20
18. Can Bears retract their claws?........................................................................21
19. Do different Bear species have different shaped claws?....................................22
20. What animal do Sloth Bears look a lot like? ....................................................23
21. Where do Sloth Bears live? ............................................................................24
22. How are Sloth Bears different from other Bears? .............................................25
23. What strange eating habits do Sloth Bears have?.............................................26
24. How much does a tiny baby Bear grow?..........................................................27
25. Where do Sun Bears get their name?..............................................................28
26. What other weird feature do Sun Bears have?.................................................29
27. What other surprises do Sun Bears have? ......................................................30
28 Where do Grizzly Bears get their name?..........................................................31
29. Where do Grizzly Bears get their fearsome reputation? ...................................32

30. How good are a Grizzly Bear's senses? ................................................33
31. How do Grizzlies prepare for their hibernation? ................................34
32. Do Grizzlies love water? ......................................................................35
33. What is South America's only Bear? ...................................................36
34. Are Spectacled Bears shy creatures? ..................................................37
35. What is one difference between Spectacled Bears and other Bears? ..........38
36. How many teeth do Bears have? .........................................................39
37. Are all American Black Bears black in color? ....................................40
38. What are the differences between Black Bears and Grizzly Bears? .............41
39. Do you know these Bear hibernating facts? ......................................42
40. Can all Bears climb? ............................................................................43
41. Of which countries are Bears the national animal? ..........................44
42. Do you know where the Teddy Bear got its name? ..........................45
43. Which famous poet kept a Bear as a pet instead of a dog? .............46
44. Do you know that Winnie the Pooh was based on a real Bear? .....47
45. Why do Bears stand on two legs? ......................................................48
46. Do you know these Bear facts? ..........................................................50
47. What about these Bear facts? ............................................................51
48. What are the only predators willing to take on a Bear? ..................52
49. Where are the car license plates shaped like Polar Bears? ..............53
50. Which USA State has an extinct Bear in its flag? ..............................54
51. Are Bears smart animals? ...................................................................55
If you liked this book…please tell others… .................................................56

# 1. How many species of Bears are there?

*A Brown Bear family - Image by Volt Collection / Shutterstock.com*

There are only 8 species of Bears living in the world today

- Giant Panda Bear
- Spectacled Bear
- Sun Bear
- Sloth Bear
- Asian Black Bear
- American Black Bear
- Brown Bear
- Polar Bear

## 2. Where do you find Bears today?

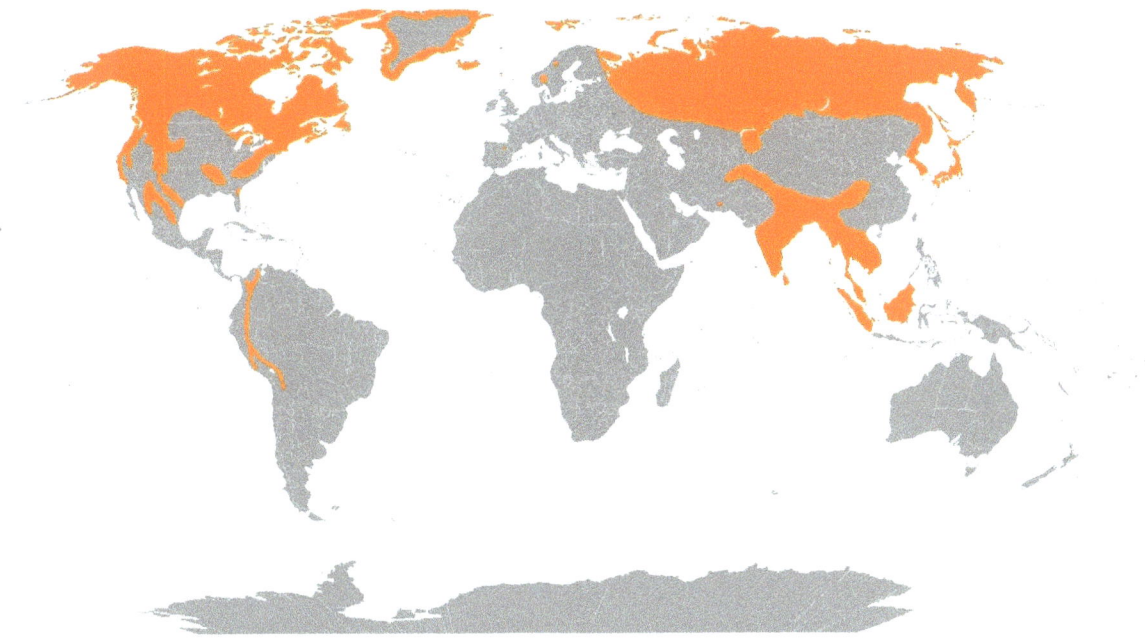

*ORANGE Areas Show where Bears live in the wild today - Public Domain*

Bears can only be found in North and South America, Asia and Europe.

There are no Bears in Africa, Australia or Antarctica.

Although Bears do not live in Africa today, Bear fossils have been found there.

## 3. How fast can Bears run?

*A running Grizzly - Photo by Malene, CC BY 2.5 / Wikimedia Commons*

Bears can run more than 40 miles per hour (60 kilometers an hour).

They run up hills, down hills or along a slope.

Bears can run more than twice as fast as we can run.

In fact, a Bear can outrun a racehorse over short distances, but has little endurance.

## 4. Is a Polar Bear's fur really white?

*A Polar Bear close up - Photo by Ansgar Walk CC-BY-SA-3.0 / Wikimedia Commons*

A Polar Bear's fur is not white.

Each hair is a clear hollow tube.

Polar Bears look white because each hollow hair reflects the light.

## 5. What color skin do Polar Bears have?

*Polar Bear on the Prowl - Photo by Alan Wilson - www.naturespicsonline.com, CC BY-SA 3.0 / Wikimedia Commons*

Polar Bears have black skin under their white fur to better absorb the rays of the sun.

Their fur is so thick with over 9,500 hairs per square inch (per 2.5 square cm) that you cannot see the color of their skin underneath their fur.

# 6. Do Polar Bears favor one giant paw over the other?

*Giant Polar Bear Paw up close - Photo by Ted / Flickr.com*

Do you have any friend who is left handed?

Tell them they are not the only ones, as all Polar Bears are left-handed.

## 7. Can the biggest Bear jump?

*Polar Bear Jumping - Arturo de Frias Marques / Flickr.com*

Polar Bears are the world's largest land predators.

When standing on its hind legs, an adult male Polar Bear may reach more than 10 feet (3 m.), and can weigh up to 1,600 pounds (725 kg).

Even though they are the biggest of all Bears, a swimming Polar Bear can jump 8 ft. (2.4 m) right out of the water to surprise a seal.

# 8. How far do Polar Bears roam?

*Polar Bear roaming - Public domain via Wikimedia Commons*

Polar Bears have the largest home ranges of any Bear.

One Polar Bear can hunt and live in an area as big as the State of Maine.

# 9. How much can a Polar Bear eat?

*A Polar Bear waiting by the water - Photo by Christopher Michel / Flickr.com*

A Polar Bear's stomach can hold 150 lbs. (68 kg) of meat.

That is the weight of 4 microwave ovens or the weight of 2 bags of cement.

# 10. How are the names "Arctic" and "Antarctic" connected to Bears?

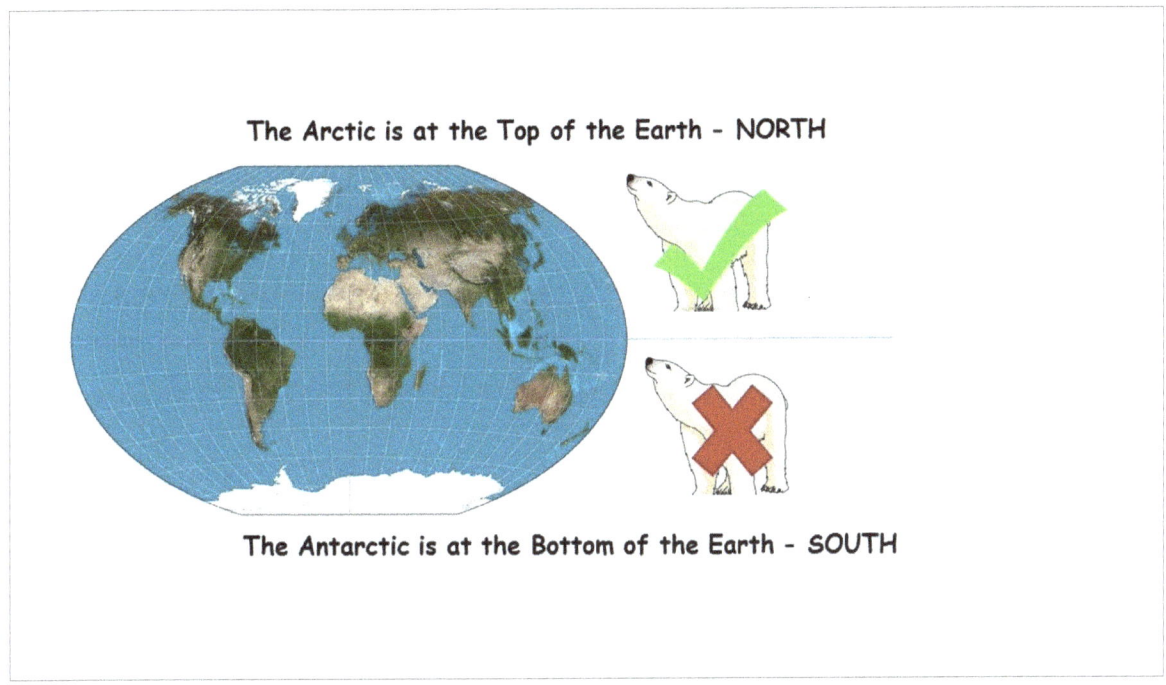

*Where Polar Bears Live in the wild today – Images -Public Domain*

Polar Bears live only in Arctic areas that surround the North Pole - not in Antarctica, which surrounds the South Pole.

In fact, the word Arctic comes from the Greek word for Bear, and Antarctic comes from the Greek meaning the opposite, without Bear.

## 11. What are the only true meat-eating Bears?

*Polar Bear eating - Photo By Paul Gierszewski /. Creativecommons.org, via Wikimedia Commons*

Only the Polar Bear is a true carnivore or meat-eater.

All other Bears are omnivores, or animals that eat both plants and meat.

Even Grizzly Bears eat mostly nuts, berries, fruit, leaves, insects and roots.

## 12. Does a Polar Bear have a cloak of invisibility?

*Polar Bear - Public Domain Photo / pixabay.com*

Two layers of fur and a thick layer of body fat provide polar Bears with such excellent insulation that their body temperature and metabolic rate won't change even when temperatures reach -34°F (-37°C).

Polar Bears have almost the same body temperature as humans - 98.6°F (37°C).

Because of their thick layers of insulation, Polar Bears don't give off any detectable heat. So they won't show up in infrared photographs.

It's almost like having a built-in cloak of invisibility!

## 13. Are Koala Bears really Bears?

*Koala Bear - Photo by Rickyd / Shutterstock.com*

Koalas are actually not Bears - they're marsupials.

Do you know that Koalas have finger prints like us? Koalas and animals that are primates like monkeys, apes and humans are the only animals who have finger prints.

# 14. Are Giant Panda Bears endangered?

*Giant Panda Bear - Photo by Harvey Barrison / Flickr.com*

In Chinese, the Panda is called 'Da Xiong Mao', meaning 'giant Bear cat'.

Giant Panda Bears are an endangered species.

There are around 1000 of them existing in the wild, and 100 of them in captivity.

At birth, a Panda is smaller than a mouse and weighs about only about four ounces (113 grams).

## 15. What human illnesses do Giant Panda Bears suffer from?

*Giant Panda Bear resting - By Rob / Flickr.com*

The only human illness that affects Pandas is chicken-pox.

# 16. What do Giant Pandas eat a ton of?

*Giant Panda Bear eating - Photo by Cliff, CC BY 2.0 / Wikimedia Commons*

Approximately 99 percent of a Panda's diet is bamboo leaves and shoots. Pandas spend 98 percent of their time eating or sleeping.

An adult Panda typically spends 12 hours a day eating and must consume 45 pounds (20 kg) of bamboo daily to fulfill its dietary needs.

The Panda sits while eating - instead of standing while eating food, the Panda will sit in order to use its front paws to hold the bamboo shoots.

## 17. Do Giant Pandas bite?

*Giant Panda Eating – Photo by Sue Cantan / Flickr.com*

Pandas have a very strong bite force---higher than tigers or lions.

They have a large round face and jaw that is filled with powerful jaw muscles to eat the tough bamboo.

They also have large molars to crush and grind the tough bamboo fibers.

## 18. Can Bears retract their claws?

*Brown Bear Paw with Claws - Photo by Luke Jones / Flickr.com*

Just like dogs, Bears have non-retractable claws.

Cats have retractable claws.

The claws on the front feet of Bears are longer than the claws on the back feet.

Some large Bears have claws almost 5 inches (12,7 cm) long.

# 19. Do different Bear species have different shaped claws?

*Bear Claws - Shannon Kringen / Flickr.com*

The shape of a Bear's claw depends on the type of Bear.

Bears that climb, such as Black Bears, have claws that are curved and strong to allow them to claw at tree bark.

Bears that dig, such as Grizzly Bears, have straight and long claws.

## 20. What animal do Sloth Bears look a lot like?

*Sloth Bear - Photo by Lara604 / Flickr.com*

The Sloth Bear has thick shaggy fur that is black to brown colored. Its ears are lined with long fur and it has a long snout, a long tongue, round eyes, and a large nose.

Its head looks like a dog. The area around it's muzzle and eyes are cream colored. The Sloth Bear has a V or U-shaped pattern displayed on its chest that is white or gold colored.

In the late 1700s, the first Europeans to see Sloth Bears described them as Bear-like sloths due to their messy appearance and long claws.

## 21. Where do Sloth Bears live?

*Sloth Bear - Photo by Lara604 / Flickr.com*

Common habitats include grasslands, forests, and dense brush lands.

They are only found in certain parts of Asia such as India, Bangladesh, Sri Lanka, Bhutan, and Nepal.

## 22. How are Sloth Bears different from other Bears?

*A mother Sloth Bear with a cub on her back - Photo by L. Shyamal / Wikimedia Commons*

Sloth Bears are the only Bears to carry young on their backs.

Unlike other species of Bears, Sloth Bears are mostly nocturnal. They sleep during the day and they look for food at night.

Sloth Bears do not hibernate due to their warmer climates and the availability of food sources throughout the year.

## 23. What strange eating habits do Sloth Bears have?

*Sloth Bear - Photo by Kim / Flickr.com*

Sloth Bears feed mainly on termites and ants.

Their long, curved claws are used to get into termite and ant nests, which can be rock-hard.

Once a Sloth Bear has opened a hole into the nest, it blows away the excess dirt.

It then sticks its snout into the hole, closes its nostrils and 'vacuums' the termites into its mouth. Its long tongue scoops up the termites that get away!

People have heard their sucking and slurping from over 300 feet (90 meters) away!

Besides termites and ants, Sloth Bears eat fruit. They love mangoes and figs.

## 24. How much does a tiny baby Bear grow?

*Kodiak Bear - Photo by S. Taheri, CC BY-SA 3.0 / Wikimedia Commons*

Kodiak Bears are one of the 2 largest of all Bears alive today.

The other is the Polar Bear. Kodiak Bears belong to the Brown Bear family.

A newly born Kodiak Bear can weigh less than 1 pound (.45 kg).

As it grows up, its weight may increase as much as 1,000 times.

Full grown Kodiak Bears can weigh up to 1500 pounds (680 kg).

If human babies grew this much, as adults they would weigh over 6,000 pounds (2,722 kg)!

# 27. What other surprises do Sun Bears have?

*Sun Bear showing its powerful teeth – Photo by J. Patrick Fischer / Wikimedia Commons*

When threatened a Sun Bear is able to make a barking sound like a dog.

They have the biggest teeth relative to their body size of any other Bear species.

Their teeth are strong enough to chew through Bellian Wood, also known as Diamond Wood, that is extremely hard and dense.

Sun Bears have the shortest fur of all Bears, so they can keep cool in the hot forests of Southeast Asia where they live.

The male Sun Bear has shorter fur than a female Sun Bear.

A Sun Bear's claws grow throughout its lifetime- you can tell a Sun Bear's age by the length of its claws.

# 28 Where do Grizzly Bears get their name?

*A Mother Grizzly and Cubs - Denali National Park and Preserve photo, CC BY 2.0 / Wikimedia Commons*

The famous explorers Lewis and Clark first gave the Bear its name — "grisly" or "grizzly".

There are 2 possible reasons for the name.

They could have named it after the golden and grey tips of hair that gave it a "grizzled" look.

Grizzly also could have meant "fear-inspiring".

Grizzlies belong to the Brown Bear family.

# 29. Where do Grizzly Bears get their fearsome reputation?

*A Big Grizzly Bear - Photo by Ken Conger - Denali National Park and Preserve / Flickr.com*

A Grizzly will fight more ferociously, and be more aggressive than any other animal, when it believes it needs to protect itself or its cubs. This is where the Grizzly gets its reputation for being so dangerous.

In more than 70% of fatal attacks on humans, a Grizzly Bear mother was defending her cubs from what she thought was danger.

Many Grizzly Bear attacks result when a Bear has been surprised by humans at very close range.

Grizzlies have such a powerful bite they could crush a bowling ball in their jaws.

# 30. How good are a Grizzly Bear's senses?

*Grizzly Bear sniffing the air - Chris Parker / Flickr.com*

A Grizzly Bear has a better sense of smell than a hunting dog.

When the wind is blowing towards them, Grizzlies can smell a dead animal from 20 miles (30 km) away.

Unlike other animals, like Cats and Dogs, Grizzlies see in full color just like humans.

Grizzlies also have excellent night vision, which is better than humans.

# 31. How do Grizzlies prepare for their hibernation?

*Grizzly Fishing - Galyna Andrushko / Shutterstock.com*

Bears have only about 7 months to eat enough food to last for the whole year.

During hibernation the Grizzly Bear doesn't eat or drink.

As Winter approaches, Bears may eat for 20-23 hours a day to store enough fat to survive through hibernation.

Grizzlies will eat up to 80 to 100 pounds (36 to 45 kg) of food per day. They are able to gain 3 to 6 pounds (1.35 to2.75 kg) in body weight in a day.

Grizzlies will eat up to 25 fish per day when they are preparing for hibernation. This is almost 20,000 calories a day.

Hibernation lasts between 5 and 8 months. During hibernation, their breathing and heart rate will slow down and they will survive only on their fat reserves.

During hibernation, a Grizzly can wake up at any time if it is disturbed.

## 32. Do Grizzlies love water?

*A Grizzly Bear swimming - Photo by Michael Fraley / Flickr.com*

Grizzlies are good swimmers. Grizzlies in coastal areas have been known to hunt seals by swimming in the sea.

Swimming across a river or a lake is easy for these Bears.

During the heat of Summer Grizzlies have been seen cooling off in water just as we humans do.

## 33. What is South America's only Bear?

*A Spectacled Bear - Photo by Tambako The Jaguar / Flickr.com*

Spectacled Bears are the only species of Bear found in South America.

Spectacled Bears are also known as Andean Bears, because they live in parts of the Andes Mountains of South America.

Spectacled Bears are an endangered species. There are as few as 3,000 remaining in the wild today.

They have thick, brown/black fur and cream colored markings on their muzzle, throat, chest and around their eyes.

The markings around their eyes gives them the appearance of wearing spectacles, giving them their name.

## 34. Are Spectacled Bears shy creatures?

*A Spectacled Bear - Photo by socialBedia / Flickr.com*

Spectacled Bears are very shy Bears, and avoid people.

They prefer the isolated forests on the slopes of the Andes, climbing as high as 14,000 feet (4,300 meters). They will descend to search for food.

Spectacled Bears are the most arboreal of all Bears. This means they live or spend a large amount of their time in trees or bushes.

## 35. What is one difference between Spectacled Bears and other Bears?

*Spectacled Bear – Photo by Nigel Swales / Flickr.com*

All other Bear species have 14 pairs of ribs, but Spectacled Bears are different.

They have only 13 pairs of ribs.

## 36. How many teeth do Bears have?

*A Brown Bear eating a bone - Photo by Steve Baker / Flickr.com*

Most Bears have 42 teeth, which is 10 more than human adults. An adult human has 32 teeth.

A Bear's canines can reach 1.5 inches (3.8 cm) long, while a human's are less than 0.5 inch (1.25 cm) long.

## 37. Are all American Black Bears black in color?

*A Cinnamon-colored Black Bear eating dandelions – Photo by Traveler100, CC BY-SA 3.0 Wikimedia Commons*

Though they are called Black Bears, the species comes in a range of colors.

Black Bears come in more colors than any other North American mammal.

They can be black, brown, cinnamon, blond, blue-gray, or white.

The variation in color has to do with their environment.

A lighter color is common in half of the Black Bears in the Western USA states.

The lighter color helps them blend in better in open meadows as well as reduces heat stress.

In the Northeast USA states, around 97% of Black Bears are black in color.

## 38. What are the differences between Black Bears and Grizzly Bears?

Left - Black Bear – by Jim Martin / Public Domain,   Right - Grizzly Bear - by chascar / Flickr.com

It is common for people to mistake Black Bears as Grizzly Bears when just looking at the color of their fur.

There are quite a few differences between Black Bears and Grizzlies.

- Black Bears are smaller.
- Black Bears don't have the bulging shoulder hump of Grizzly Bears.
- Black Bears have a narrower, straight face.
- Black Bears have taller ears than Grizzly Bears.
- Black Bears have shorter claws than Grizzly Bears.

# 39. Do you know these Bear hibernating facts?

*Bear den – Photo by Andreas Argirakis / Shutterstock.com*

Not all Bears hibernate. Asian Black Bears, American Black Bears, some Brown Bear species, and pregnant Polar Bears hibernate.

Sloth Bears live in warm places with plenty of food, so they don't need to hibernate.

A Bear's normal heartbeat is 40 beats per minute. A hibernating Bear's heart rate drops to 8 beats per minute.

During hibernation, a Bear does not poop.

Its body can somehow recycle body waste into protein—a process that scientists still do not understand.

Hibernating female Bears have their babies during hibernation in mid-winter.

Bear mothers nurse their babies in the den until spring arrives.

## 40. Can all Bears climb?

*Black Bear climbing - Photo by California Department of Fish and Wildlife / Flickr.com*

Black Bears are far better at climbing trees than other Bear species, but all species of Bears can climb trees when they need to.

A common misconception is that Grizzly Bears cannot climb trees.

While its long claws make climbing more difficult and slower, a Grizzly can still climb trees

Even Polar Bears can climb rocks and some have been known to climb trees in zoos.

## 41. Of which countries are Bears the national animal?

Bears are the national animals of 3 countries – China, Finland and Russia.

*Left to Right - Flags of China, Finland and Russia - Public Domain / Wikimedia Commons*

The Giant Panda is the national animal of China.

The Brown Bear is the national animal of both Finland and Russia.

## 42. Do you know where the Teddy Bear got its name?

*A Teddy Bear – Photo by Antranias / Pixabay.com*

In November 1902, President Theodore Roosevelt and some of his friends went on a hunting trip. They could not find any adult Bears to shoot.

Eventually they tracked down and surrounded a helpless Bear cub. The President refused to shoot the cub.

Soon after, a newspaper cartoonist drew a cartoon showing Roosevelt saving the Bear cub.

When a store owner in New York saw the cartoon, he decided to make toy Bears to sell in his shop. He asked President Roosevelt for permission to use the name "Teddy's Bear" for his stuffed Bear toys, as a reminder of the Bear cub that President Roosevelt saved.

Today everyone knows these toys as Teddy Bears, but few people know that they were named after President Theodore "Teddy" Roosevelt. "Teddy" was the President's nickname.

## 43. Which famous poet kept a Bear as a pet instead of a dog?

*Lord Byron painting - By Richard Westall - National Portrait Gallery -Wikimedia Commons*

The famous poet Lord Byron was a pet lover.

In 1805, when he became a student at Trinity College, Cambridge University, the college authorities told him that pet dogs were not allowed.

So he decided to buy a tame Bear instead.

He argued that Bears were not specifically mentioned as not being allowed to be kept as a pet in the rules of the college.

Byron won the argument against the college and the Bear stayed with him in his college rooms.

## 44. Do you know that Winnie the Pooh was based on a real Bear?

*The real "Winnie" Bear Cub with her owner - Manitoba Provincial Archives, Public Domain*

In 1914, Canadian Lieutenant Harry Colebourn bought a Bear cub from a hunter for $20 in Ontario, Canada. He was on his way to England to fight in the First World War.

He named the Bear "Winnie" after his hometown of Winnipeg, Manitoba.

Colebourn brought "Winnie" to England with him, but he had to leave "Winnie" at the London Zoo while his army unit were fighting in France during the war.

"Winnie" became a much loved attraction at the London Zoo. After the war ended, "Winnie" was officially donated to the zoo.

The writer A. A. Milne used to take his son Christopher Robin Milne to the London Zoo, where he often saw the real "Winnie".

Christopher Robin Milne named his toy Bear "Winnie" and his dad (A.A. Milne) named the character in his books "Winnie-the-Pooh" after Christopher's teddy bear.

## 45. Why do Bears stand on two legs?

*Grizzly Bear and 2 cubs standing - Photo by Gleb Tarro / Shutterstock.com*

Bears can see, hear, and smell better standing up than they can when they are down on all four legs.

So, when they are standing up they are just trying to see what is in front of them.

Cubs especially stand up a lot just to see over the grass.

While Bears are able to stand and walk on their hind legs, they usually stand or walk on all four legs.

Bears are bowlegged. This gives them better grip and balance when they stand and walk.

Just like humans, Bears stand and walk on the soles of their feet rather than on their toes.

Most other mammals like Horses, Elephants, Dogs and Cats walk on their toes.

Because Bears can walk short distances on their hind legs, some Native Americans called them "the beast that walks like a man."

## 46. Do you know these Bear facts?

*Mother Bear and 3 Cubs - Arend / Flickr.com*

- A male Bear is called a boar or a "he-bear". A female Bear is called a sow or a "she-bear".

- A group of Bears is called a sloth. One could say, "I was at the river and saw a sloth of Bears fishing."

- Bears have been known to eat almost anything, including snowmobile seats, engine oil, and rubber boots.

## 47. What about these Bear facts?

*A Polar Bear Swimming Underwater - By Jonathan Griffiths, CC BY-SA 3.0 via Wikimedia Commons*

- Polar Bears are strong swimmers and are known to dive underwater to sneak up to catch seals. The longest recorded dive by a Polar Bear that remained underwater was 3 minutes and 10 seconds. How long do you think you could hold your breath underwater?

- Polar Bears can swim over 60 miles (96 km) without stopping.

- If you eat a Polar Bear liver, you'll die. Seals are the main source of food for Polar Bears and the major reason for their high levels of vitamin A. Humans can't handle that much vitamin A.

- Most Bears are born without fur. Only Polar Bears and Giant Pandas are born with thin white fur.

## 48. What are the only predators willing to take on a Bear?

*A Bengal Tiger - Soren Wolf / Flickr.com*

In Asia, a large Tiger might sometimes kill and eat a small or medium-size Panda or other Asian Bear.

Anywhere else in the world, the only animal that can eat a full-grown Bear is another Bear.

Bears sometimes do eat other Bears.

Baby Bears have the most to fear from other Bears.

Large male Grizzly Bears occasionally kill and eat Grizzly Bear cubs. And large male Polar Bears sometimes kill and eat small Polar Bears.

Bear cubs are preyed upon by Cougars, Bobcats and Coyotes.

Sometimes Grizzly Bears kill Black Bears. A full-grown Grizzly is much larger and stronger than the largest Black Bear. So, Black Bears always try to escape when they see a Grizzly.

## 49. Where are the car license plates shaped like Polar Bears?

*Polar Bear Shaped North West Territories License Plate - Jerry "Woody" / Flickr.com*

Two territories in Canada have license plates that display Polar Bears in some way.

The North West Territory has a license plate that is shaped like a Polar Bear.

The Territory of Nunavut has a Polar Bear in the background of their license plates.

*Polar Bear license plate from Nunavut Territory - By Awmcphee (Own work) [CC0], via Wikimedia Commons*

## 50. Which USA State has an extinct Bear in its flag?

*State of California's Official Flag - By Devin Cook, Public Domain / Wikimedia Commons*

The first official version of the Bear Flag was adopted by the State of California under Governor Hiram Johnson in 1911.

The California Grizzly was declared the official state animal in 1953.

California 's official state animal, the California Grizzly Bear, is actually extinct.

The last California Grizzly was seen in the Sierra Madre Mountains (Santa Barbara County) in 1924. Since then Grizzlies have never been seen in the wild again in California.

# 51. Are Bears smart animals?

*A Bear deep in thought - Metassus / Flickr.com*

Bears are considered by many wildlife biologists to be one of the most intelligent land animals of North America.

Bears have the largest and most complex brains relative to their size of any land mammal. In the animal kingdom, their intelligence compares with that of higher primates, like Chimpanzees.

Bears can perform complex tasks — a sign that they are able to learn and process information. Bears have been trained to balance on balls, ride roller skates, and play sports and musical instruments. Zookeepers and animal trainers believe Bears are smarter than Dogs. Bears have been known to roll rocks into Bear traps to set off the trap and eat the bait without getting caught in the trap.

Bears also have great memories. They can remember where they found food even if they visited the place years ago. They can remember pathways from years ago and can recognize other animals from years ago too.

## If you liked this book...please tell others...

If you liked this book, please leave a review at the bookseller website where you purchased this book. Please tell others what you liked about this book.

**Visit www.TJRob.com for a FREE eBook and to see TJ Rob's other exciting books**

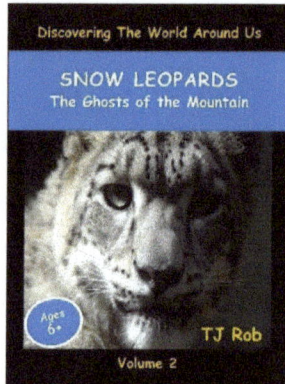
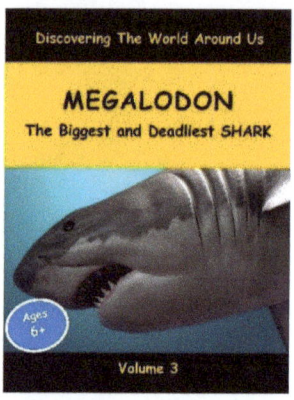
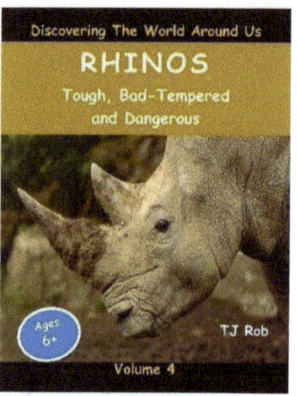
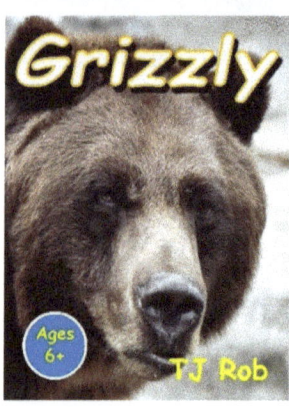
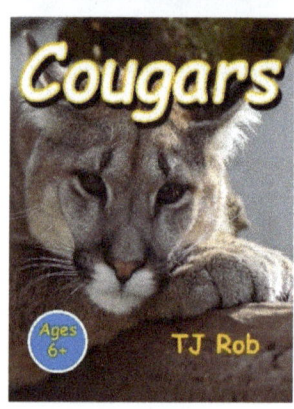

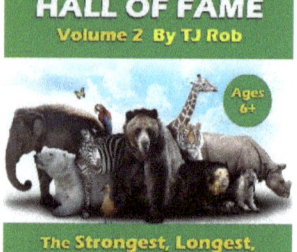
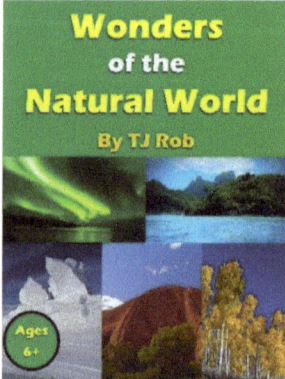
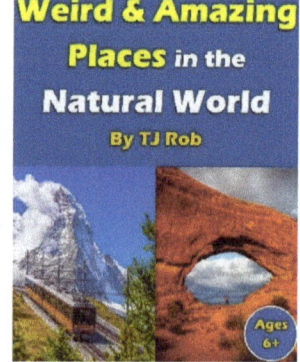

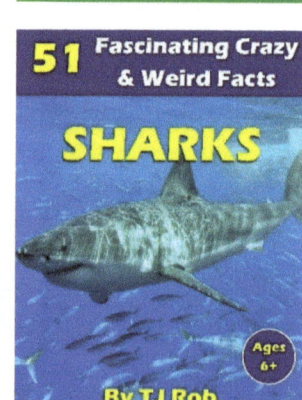

www.ingramcontent.com/pod-product-compliance
Lightning Source LLC
Chambersburg PA
CBHW040003080526
44586CB00027B/2868